Greetings from

Ocean Grove

NEW JERSEY

Ocean Grove

SUMMER

Childhood Memories of Ocean Grove

Illustrated by Sue Anderson Gioulis

Written by Kathryn Hess

KFR
COMMUNICATIONS

Ocean Grove Summer

Published by: KFR Communications, LLC

Publisher's Note: The author and publisher have taken care in preparation
of this book but make no expressed or implied warranty of any kind and
assume no responsibility for errors or omissions. No liability is assumed for
incidental or consequential damages in connection with or arising out of the
use of the information contained herein.

ISBN-10: 1939406099
ISBN-13: 978-1-939406-09-5

Printed in the United States of America

www.kfrcommunications.com

*Joy is the most infallible sign
of the presence of God.*

-Pierre Teihard de Chardin

This book is dedicated to
Karen Riley
who loved Ocean Grove

God's Square Mile,
His sea shore smile.

A glow from the ocean becomes the sun.
Our summer here has finally begun.

Crawling from my bed,
I find streets lined with Gingerbread.

A morning walk will fill our sails,
as we head to the beach with our shovels and pails.

For sea shells and stones we make a careful inspection,
finding just the right ones for our collection.

At noon we have lunch of sandwiches with baloney.
For dessert there is crumb cake,
although sometimes we have spumoni.

An afternoon tour shows Great Auditorium spires.
And a sign says there will soon be a Festival of Choirs.

We find Tenters at the heart of this wonderful town.
They live under canvas that never falls down.

There are colorful striped awnings and infinite flowers,
porches to sit on for quiet summer hours.

A chapel called Thornley

and Bishop Janes Tabernacle,

It's the 4th of July weekend
with fireworks that crackle.

The Young People's Temple

and Beersheba's well,
we have a sip of water and walk back to our hotel.

Before dusk we ride bicycles from Inskip to Spray,
and stop to meet friends on Pilgrim Pathway.

Many days have passed since that first morning light.
And I feel that I have grown, although not much in height.

I have learned to find joy in the simplest things.
I've heard wondrous music and Auditorium bells ring.

But most DAYS here I sincerely dream,

that I can fi-NAGLE a chocolate ice cream.

An ugly duckling grew up, and came out of hide-in.
Because he became a swan, that everyone could ride in.

Tomorrow we will leave, but today we are here.
I dance in the waves and it's perfectly clear,
I want to always come here and live on this land,
where each day I can squish my toes in the sand.

Looking now to the west over the Boardwalk Pavilion,
the sun casts the sky in the softest vermillion.

I love Ocean Grove, it is my safe place,
my real home, my amazing grace.

Sue Anderson Gioulis (left) had her formal training at the Ringling College of Art and Design in Sarasota, Florida. Her illustrations are featured in a number of children's books and she is a member of the Manasquan River Group of Artists. Her artwork is shown at the Main Avenue Galleria in Ocean Grove or online at www.suelynanderson.com.

Kathryn Hess (right) is an artist living in Brick, New Jersey. She enjoys writing and is an avid reader. Spirituality, psychology, world and local history, are also important focuses in her life. She graduated from Linden Hall and Millersville University earning an MS in Psychology.

Made in the USA
Middletown, DE
21 September 2017